161 259117 3

Two week

D0120927

Runners in the Margins

Runners in the Margins

Poems

Akira Tatehata

Translated by Hiroaki Sato

3 0 APR 2004

895.615
T

This book is dedicated to
Aiko, Keiko, and Nancy

Except for the translator's name throughout and the poet's name on the cover and title page, all Japanese names are given the Japanese way, family name first.

Most of the translations are made by permission of Shichōsha, Tokyo, which has published Tatehata's three books of poems: *Yohaku no Runner* (Runners in the Margins, 1991), *Sono Humming o shimo* (Even That Humming, 1993), and *Patrick Seiki* (The Patrick Century, 1996). One of the uncollected poems, "*Enjin no Yume*" (Dream of a Circle), appeared in the daily *Asahi Shimbun*, another, "Siren Who Disappeared," in the Urawa Museum catalogue, *Yūten · Shi to Chōkoku ni yoru.*

Set in 11/14 Galliard, this book is printed on acid-free Domtar opaque vellum.

Copyright © 2003 by Tatehata Akira
All rights reserved

Printed in the United States of America
Cover design by Nancy Rossiter
Text design by Write Stuff Communications

Library of Congress Control Number: 2003103174
ISBN: 1-889087-09-2

P.S., A Press
169 Garron Road
Middletown Springs, VT 05757
Phone/Fax: (802) 235-2844

Contents

Preface

Tatehata Akira is a poet as well as an art critic and curator. Born in Kyoto in 1947, he wanted to become a physicist but when he saw Federico Fellini's *8 1/2* he gave up the idea of becoming a scientist and studied French literature. Upon graduation from Waseda University, he jointed the editorial staff of the art magazine *Geijutsu Shinchō* (New Tide in Art). While on the staff, he was attracted to visual and concrete poetry. The first visual poem he wrote saw print in 1973 in *docs*, a poetry magazine published in Marseille. In 1976 he joined the Agency for Cultural Affairs and worked with a team to create the National Museum of Art, in Osaka. He stayed with the agency for fifteen years, organizing a number of contemporary art shows. Among the most recent exhibitions for which he served as curator were Yokohama Triennial 2001 and Busan (Korea) Biennale 2002. He also was the advisor and catalogue text writer for the Kusama Yayoi Retrospective at the Museum of Modern Art, New York, in 1998.

Toward the end of the 1980s, Tatehata's poems began to appear in the poetry monthly *Gendaishi Techō* (Notebook for Modern Poetry). In 1991, the year he joined the faculty of Tama Art University, he published his first book of poems, *Yohaku no Runner* (Runners in the Margins). It won the Rekitei New Poet Prize. His second, *Sono Humming o shimo* (Even That Humming), appeared in 1993 and his third, *Patrick Seiki* (The Patrick Century), in 1996.

What makes Tatehata's poetry, mostly written in "prose," unique? His fellow poets seem to agree on one point: absence of narrative. Thus Irizawa Yasuo posits that in his poetry Tatehata "early on abandoned [any attempt to achieve] commonsensical coherence of description or logic." Takahashi Mutsuo thinks what "moves Tatehata's prose poems" is "the energy or directionality of words themselves." And Inakawa Masato speaks of "the externality of 'narrative' (and the device 'to narrate') as the other" in characterizing Tatehata's poems. This disjunctive quality, if we can call it that, evokes for Takahashi the image of a poet engaged in "an idealistic, solitary activity," and it makes for a certain difficulty.

But Tatehata's aim is not to be simply abstruse. Like much of modern art, his poetry is full of allusions and references, some of which are humorous. To name only a few English literary figures he alludes to, there are James Joyce, Ezra Pound, T.S. Eliot, and Williams Carlos Williams, and like them, he likes to deploy wordplays. In fact, he is a fan of palindromes. As he tells us in one article, a young woman introduced to him years ago for an arranged marriage, which didn't work out, was a natural palindromist. Palindromes are easier in Japanese, a language full of vowels, than in English, a language full of consonants, and in any case can't be translated. So, for some I have used English substitutes. I'm delighted to note that at least one palindrome in these translations is Tatehata's own, created in English for this book.

Translated here are all of his first book, excerpts from his two others, and several poems not yet collected in a book. One of the uncollected is "Siren Who Disappeared," a poem he wrote for a collaborative work with the sculptor Muraoka Saburō for a exhibition attempting to "merge" poetry and sculpture. Muraoka incorporated the English translation made for that show in a huge "book" he fashioned out of iron. The exhibition was held at Urawa Museum from November 2002 to February 2003. The poem, both the original and the translation, was printed in the exhibition catalogue, *Yūten · Shi to Chōkoku ni yoru* (Merging Point · Through Poetry and Sculpture).

Since Tatehata was in New York as a visiting scholar at Columbia University when I translated these poems, I had the unusual luxury of going over the translations with the poet. And as always, Nancy Rossiter and Robert Fagan helped me improve the translations. Linda Peavy and Ursula Smith, the publishers of this book, meticulously edited them. I am grateful to all of them.

Hiroaki Sato
New York City

Runners in the Margins
(complete)

The Delays of Travel

I have no memory of traveling alone. I laughed at the endless hand-washing, its fierceness, but that, too, was merely someone else's shame. Slow travel in which I pile up false quotations. The slowness of prose.

Milk is white the way frosted glass is; a transparent liquid turns white when innumerable scars are made, I was told. Also, that individual is another name for a group and that it is a corrupt group, besides. (We were being laughed at.) Individualist, what do you think of the delays of travel? Are you ashamed of its "pretended irrationality"? Or are you proud? (Laugh, if you want to.) Even a man with a thin frame is, in bed, a penile warrior. Repeatedly, time and again, he stirs himself up like that. Pile up a liquid's wounds, prose on the desk, be late. Laugh at someone else's shame, a group with another name, be late. Toward daybreak, the milk, too, is black. In your memory, that dark point that touches the other. In the darkness of the quotation, prose is left behind.

A Woman Whose Diarrhea Doesn't Stop

That's the house of a woman whose diarrhea doesn't stop. No stand of trees around it, a red road quietly turns somewhere near it. I go closer, tomorrow's rain doesn't stop today either, and I, beating my thin breast, alone threaten the gray sky. The nights in which I repeated ridiculous gestures for you and laughed, those nights are now a thing of the past. The black market that nurtures dogmatic moralists appears to be no longer held in this neighborhood. As for the late-night wind that supported roadside lust, the station building with a fountain, the dark-green bench, the clattering shutters, I might forget them. But, finger pointed, I still can love only stereotypical things. A red road without any trees. The rain doesn't stop. That is the house of the woman whose diarrhea doesn't stop.

Mankind Pressing the Grass

A middle-aged woman's gigantic hip bulging out of a trifoliate orange hedge. A girl on an inclining lawn. A young woman in a barn. Ah that pressure on the grass *is* mankind's female mold. There mankind's scream is eternally molded. Do you know the term "pleasure crime"? For a disease that in the end never heals, the fuse is ignited, and the fire, having crawled over somewhere near the ham and the dent in the waist, rushes headlong to the middle of the town lights for the preservation of a trivial place-name. I gather that's what's called a "pleasure crime." I don't care for it. I have no interest in sick men. What I love is the stereotypical way women of various ages hold their hips, as well as the foliage, stands of trees, straw, clumps of grass which are appropriate for them. The true fun of mankind is consumed there, and in its place the scream is bred deep inside. That's why, at any time, mankind pressing the grass is lonesome. So I go out for a walk. It's a walk of nameless mankind.

Young Woman's Voice

About the young woman's voice. It's in the morning that it's important. In the morning, whatever nuances we may have are lost. A refreshing wind travels through a stand of trees, and in the distant plaza there appear to be some cheerful fights. At such a time it's useless to think about anything. Seated in a plywood chair, we hear a toneless and yet incredibly bright woman's voice. *Plywood chair. Young woman's voice.* And. Last night's cruel or base sleep, of the men living separated. The night wind, the morning wind, that blows through the teeth. And. The flat faces of those who practice trivial miracles. Young women's voices from downstairs, from next-door, from the hallway. In the morning, we can hear them without lust. I don't hate that much the mass of men who go out to such-and-such a place; they aren't as unseemly as you say they are, a "voice" said. Ah, clean young woman. In the morning, we don't have so much of the nuances. In the morning, surely, even a man with his skull dented (in a fight in the past) can walk a road lined with trees. That's why what's important is the morning. That is why what's important is the morning.

Half-Rising Woman

Woman who is half-rising now, who will be half-rising forever. Half-rising woman who, depending on the angle that touches on the memory, is said to reform the frame, narrow the sky, make the trees tilt, and finally fuse the mountainside and the surface of the water. I have yet to laugh at her frame and figure. Soft woman who never ends her life in a rectangular frame. Firm, pale woman. Are you scooping the water or just wetting your hands? For whom will you raise your face? Haven't you been loved? Your hands are free but turned inward, and by your profile, I, too, reform the flame.

Ambiguous Architecture

Because salvation floats up at an unexpected angle, we might as well recognize the outline of an inadequate hand toward the lower end. It appears that everything heads toward ambiguity. Like wife's illness, or else like architecture. In the event, we must give shape to them and correctly finish whatever we must finish. The end of a portable bed. Or the end of a chair that's beside it. At times a shrimp may float up near the ceiling, but never mind, because the history of interiors has miserable constraints and at the same time comes with "exile toward generality." Terrible: the walls and the hallways. The closer I get, the farther they recede. Wife who moves herself to the surroundings. What ambiguous architecture! I close my eyes and touch the inadequate hand, but it is also the outline of the hand I touch. Suddenly I open my eyes. And kill the hand, and another, for the one who laughs at this deficiency.

Address

Overseas. It is no more than a line of address to us. To the one who works at that line, we send a thin machine. I say thin, but the *jaggedness* it brings to the body is sparklingly clear. A scarlet rainbow faintly appears in its surroundings and, alongside the outline of the figure, a semi-transparent winged insect often flies. The contract contained several ambiguous items, but we skillfully overcame them. For example, it said that a machine may never make any repeat sound but must grow little by little. You may think it is a hard requirement, but there was nothing to it. We first removed every kind of rotational movement and shuttle movement and, in its place, incorporated some plants into the structure. In terms of expenses, it even worked better for us.

The machine, already packed, is waiting for shipment in the hallway. The desire for *jaggedness* surely is holding its breath in its thin box. There is no hesitation. Overseas. It is merely a line of address to us.

The Field Page

You, undulate. You, laugh. You, solidify. And voice quavering, you go out of the dark walls. —To which place?

The I of the future was weaving cells in a narrow room with sounds. The river in the room (there someone else's blood) goes on meandering but in the end never goes outside the walls. In this case, the walls are effective. But many people are thinking the opposite: one must show "a merciless attitude when push comes to shove," if possible like a fart released into the field. Did you laugh now?

Listen. What I open is a field page, where "towers of breasts" rise and I, as kith and kin of a man with someone else's blood circulating in him, and without any responsibility, am listening to a scream from an ancient age. Or to the melancholy wing-beat of a corny future cell.

Even if the meandering is a form of humiliation, listen, have no mercy when push comes to shove! You, undulate. You, laugh. You, solidify. And voice quavering, you go out of the dark walls. —To which place?

Red Dark Domain

I knew your voice. The red dark domain under the skin, where I was once derided and, even worse, hated. I think your voice still remains in the house people stopped visiting, though I don't know when, and, though I can't really grasp whether it is a photograph, a painting, porcelain, a letter, the smell of rubber, a buried seal, the pulsing darkness, or a cold request as a different matter, but in any case it belongs to the red dark domain between bones and skin.

It is a quaver and a squeak. Therefore it passes by.

I was told that the essence of being a monk is spasm, therefore they too lose their color.

Now the only thing I can do is to place my expectations in a large woman who has gotten away from the lake water and has her elbow bent in a small room. A different matter like that is cruel, too, but landscape and architecture teach us that the borderline between what's visible and what's invisible is ambiguous. Derided or hated, I withdraw into a castle of ludicrous gestures like a quaking monk. And look for the voice that is left. Under the skin, is the domain still red and dark?

Oh the Pasture Is Green

The pasture is green, oh the pasture is green. An age you explore and locate with your cold fingertips, stretching your pale hand over the tatami in the dark room, oh the pasture is green. Once, we sat side by side on wooden chairs, thinking of wounded naked bodies, trying to learn how to tie figures, how to sketch them. The lineage that leads from idealist lawn to tribal rope, also to the pulley, the gray pillar, the tribe on the wall. Or vice versa. There was once an age that had no guards or dialectics, which, in a word, could be formed with letters of protest.

Someone says "Violet." At times that's enough. But someone says "Violence." Say "Violate." At times, on the tatami, your fingertips generalize the age like that and transmit it. You stretch your pale hand, the room with no guards, the tatami with no conversation on it, oh the pasture is green. If it's letters of protest, it may be white water, Caesar's plywood chairs. Or vice versa. The tribal fingers may reach the ancient walls. "Ouch, it's cold, banished with potsherds."

Foliage Plant

When your hair is illuminated by the evening sun, all the E. T.s come together. Because it was a pleasant living room with a large window, our satellites stopped fighting, parked under Benjamin leaves, and waited for the time of the ecstatic ocean that was to emerge soon. With provisions, no worries. If you have no worries, the bright setting sun is even more beautiful. Comrades of the satellites under the Benjamin leaves. Or soldiers hiding in the *pothos*. The name of the foliage plant may change (with the ages), but because the room is bright enough, don't overlook the shine of the hair. We don't need to wait for the snake's proposition; the ancient period started long ago. The doves for peace are circling in the pot. Perennial blue. Rubber leaves. Fly over there, too. The dried bull is a noontime attribute, but I won't say too much about it. Walk the diagonal line. At the bottom of the basket pale flowers must be lying shattered. What's pinned to the wooden door must be (the hand of) a student. Oh sure! With provisions, no worries. With no worries, don't blame the foliage plant. When your hair stands out in the evening sun, all the E. T.s come together.

Runners in the Margins

Football long after Picasso. Just running isn't the right thing to do, but in our case, we are mindlessly roaming the white field. That pole. That bar. That line. Looking at them askance, they're more like a white dream. Not knowing the location of our lust, that's our defect we'd hesitate to record in our personal notes. We, the runners in the margins, won't even be able to laugh with a wife in a Baroque salon. But that the haze-like light is "trembling," it was confided to me. Also that, if you roam, it's "the immediate experience of a hidden memory." First quake. Then the lust will automatically show its outlines. . . .

Football long after Picasso. That pole, that bar, that line. My uncle who has the distant cheers seeped into his alpaca coat is also walking across the salon, but to us who see him off, eyes tending to be shyly lowered, the act also is like a white dream.

Yes, we are runners in the margins.

"There is a historic body lifted above this beautiful field."

We are quaking runners in the margins.

"The honeybee's wing-beat is the figure of a flower's lust."

Different Opinion

The dinosaurs are green. And they, parent and child, walk past the window of the afternoon classroom, their faces side by side, or so I hear. Oh, what an inadequate explanation! I have a different opinion, which is far more beautiful. Rather than look, be looked at. Self-consciousness that has generated like vapor on a fine day, let it be the oxygen in the yard. Our backs are green. We are afternoon dinosaurs.

Short Venetians. Narrow-faced Sydneyites. Firm muscles lodge in those women's calves. Among them is the daughter of an inn who has boarded a plane with a rolled-up drawing. "The qualification to live on" is something like that. Grasp them, and her calves are firm, but you, too, are afternoon dinosaurs. You may be dissatisfied and crouch. But even beside the wall the prophesy ought to be fulfilled. Those women are a brilliant different opinion; the age "that keeps you waiting" has ended.

Rather than look, be looked at,. That is the secret teaching of the afternoon class. *Il conte, per favore.* I am forty-two years old.

Godzilla of the Distance

Because you cannot sleep adequately, remain in the embrace of the sad shadow of a tree that is me. There is a distance, says everyone. Everybody picks up a video camera and goes to the plaza. Just as I thought, my back is a passage. Let me concoct something like the conversations they're having there. *Aura's Paradox, Godzilla's Counterattack* are fun stories which, if explained, can lead to swearing and curses. "Sarcasm is an art." "I've met you at a time in my life when I'm neither here nor there."

—I once read a "how-to book." After love, you should sleep a little. "Doesn't this look funny?" "That's the sound of the wind. An awfully regular sound." —Yes, that's the sound of the wind that blows at a time in your life when you're neither here nor there. Everybody picks up a video camera and goes to the plaza to ascertain styles of life, and that's called Aura's paradox. "Everyone wants to erase the distance." "Well, I am Godzilla, then. I like the distance." —Ah, that's why you can't sleep well. Small Godzilla, Godzilla of the distance, for now remain in the embrace of the shadow of a tree that is me.

The Voice and the Treaty: I

There's no one who laughs at the light. Because everything exists for the treaty, now count on the semi-transparent wings and fly from that tower to this cobbled road, hoping for the collapse of the administration. You've already ceased to exist. Not even your legs remain. Except, even now the voice is circulating in the night sky. If I am to contemplate somewhat on blood, you drained the wings of blood to maintain the treaty. The town darkened, and it was about that time that people stopped laughing at the light. And now politics profoundly occupies the sky.

The Voice and the Treaty: II

From today on I decided to allocate the afternoon hours to research titular things. Under the table brightened as fire are your legs that are cut apart. But I'll never despair. I, with a pale face, research titular things. It was once ambiguously called a "treaty." Because afterward the organ (organism?) blackened like an insect that doesn't grow wings, it came to be regarded ambiguously as a symbol by the individualists' usual method. But don't make a mistake. It isn't a "scream." I won't despair. Brightening the table like fire, I study titular things. On your legs that are cut apart. The summer 1987. Life as a style.

The Power of the Grass and the Black Suit

If it's the personal notes of a man who battled the power of the grass, I'll read it. Be it Baroque or a dark spaceship, the place of pleasure is momentary. That incline to the moat is no longer visible, but I won't talk about the period that ended. Nor about tomorrow! The black suit arched like a bow, and the *mesh* hat rolled. That is fact, on the day recorded in the personal notes as "Yotsuya" or "Tsukiji." From where does the loneliness emerge? And why is it repeated? The power of the grass and the black suit. The power of the grass and, the black suit.

A Foul Habit

For the vehicle called a horse carriage, many incidents, love affairs, and dresses and landscapes were imagined, but a past like that seems altogether useless to me. The same is true of things like a boat. Nowhere is a distance that deserves to be called next-door. It is also difficult to search for water plants. So I head for a certain "land owned by a woman friend." Or for "land owned by a woman friend's woman friend." With these legs for which it has become a foul habit to count the steps.

A Youth Who Can't Shit

If there's a youth who can't shit, let me know. I'd like to have him talk about how much fun life is. Will he contentedly respond by saying that situated in "a special site, an actual site" like the equestrian statue of Marcus Aurelius in the Campidoglio, he is repeating great failures? Will he gallantly assert that he doesn't even know the difference between autonomous and autocratic? Or will he overbearingly tell us that soon (that is, as the twentieth century draws to a close) "category" becomes vague and the shit he can't shit comes out and that's even more of a failure? But! But! But! The axiom of shame is iconography. The matter of shit is historicism. To a statue, life may be too hard.

Groove and Context

There's no one who laughs at narrowness. Paulownia trees and long-bodied young men all exist materially and are unaccustomed to moves like suddenly running away. I turn behind your back and ascertain the narrowness. It's softer than you are. And. I now have no history. (Why can't you laugh at this narrowness?)

If it's hard, use your hands. Massaging your long body, I think of that cold context which in the end didn't detach itself from things. I look for history with my fingertips. It's a groove that gets narrower. The dirty organ held in mouth, I trace the groove. Grapes. I'm going back? Don't laugh.

That Parrot, This Carrot

I will not fight for you. Because the sun will set soon, shooting stars will be seen from west to east. The premonitions will all be fulfilled. It is ludicrous if you think you can take care of everything with a narrow society or an anti-society. To think grumbling is confrontation and regard dull rhetoric as history, if it's a right to laugh off such a worn-out contest, everyone has it. Though it's a terrible morning, I open the window, compare that parrot with this carrot, and inch toward the one-man show that wasn't fulfilled yesterday. Insincerity is my habit. The night is far, and near. You are fundamentally miserable on account of your hobby of being criticized, but I'd rather ask for non-criticism. You being no longer young, know that you are in a process that hasn't begun and is already ending. Because the sun will set soon, you can see shooting stars. Though, as to now, it's a truly terrible morning that makes me flinch from the battle of sitting down on a chair of cold pipes. Though it's a really terrible morning, when outside the window there's only a dirty plaza, both that parrot and this carrot stone-cold.

The Running Nose, the Hanzōmon Line
Is Non-linear

I don't understand noses. When finding fault with them started, why it degenerated into formalism, why I ended up attacking them unthinkingly, even though I didn't really dislike them, whether, whatever it may be, it is the so-called centripetal force of impotence in developmental psychology that shuns linear things, there are many things I don't understand. The nose is for the nose, they say. The nose's independent system squeezes its way through the congregation of truth, good, and beauty and, squeezing its way, runs past Kudanshita. The kinetic of impotence, which in the end doesn't maldistribute someone else's blood, should be appreciated. The lamentist's running nose is ludicrous but great. Come October, about the nose, will I understand it? If I understand, will I run? If I run, the subway, be it Hanzōmon or Jimbō-chō, whichever, will firm up its preference for non-linearness. If paradox is unable to attain truth, was my behavior without understanding unthinking? —the running nose, the Hanzōmon Line is non-linear.

Anti-annotation

to Kitutsuji Yoshihisa

\<Cherry · Gift>

Because the sealed *dessin* was delivered, he closed shut the pipe by the wall following that evil promise. That is why birds shrank and flowers stopped time. As for him, he hid himself in our memory, but that, too, may be a trick of the "historical present."

\<Door>

The door of closed legs.

The snow's saliva.

\<Olive · Prayer>

Everyone is about to forget that the tree once had a human form. His gentle fingers hiding an iron mask behind the tree secretly touch that taboo. If we are intimidated by the darkness of the width of the eyes, of the one praying opening them narrowly, we will still remember the meaning of the other. Look into the mirror under the sentimental olive branches. Even what is called "I" is no more than a remembrance.

\<Gasification>

Air-burial. Painting is said to paint the air; or it may be to seal sensibilities in the air. That's why the particles are forever swaying and moving while burying softly what lies above the past.

<Paulownia · Bag of Haze>

It is cruel. What's left is always beautiful. Even if it were an evil scheme. No, the malice for a small piece of paper or a feather was a hobby termed by the deceased sage meaningless, an uncompensated malice, or was it? If I may say more, it is the remains of an incident of non-being, a masterless thing left under paulownia leaves.

<Apple · Bubbles of Light>

Starting to talk always after the story is over is the bad habit of his text. There must be appropriate etiquette for pretending fiction toward fiction. Looking up the apple branches, we grope for memories that can't possibly be, but it's just that we were distracted by the ascending vertical angle and taken advantage of. But this incline suddenly make us solitary. And during the unthinking moments before you turn to look are "words" born. *I am the other.*

The Storehouse and a Chanson

That afternoon, the man who realized he was behind, it is said, chiseled the rabbit's ear to catch up. This appears to have provoked resentment among his family members. The next day the rabbit with one ear was again brought before the man in the guestroom. Perhaps thinking it was too late, no matter what he did, that middle-aged man went into the next room and hummed a chanson he barely remembered.

"Without plans, without habits, we can dream about our lives."

The papered doors shone white, reflecting the morning sun, and the young woman who was to become his second wife, who ran after him with the rabbit in her arms, hesitated.

"Everything is possible. Everything is permitted."

The peaceful hour was eternally chiseled along with the pitiable ear. Sooner or later, the storehouse will have to be given up.

If you're middle-aged, say you're middle-aged. You don't have to be ashamed; the day will pass.

"Come, I'm over there. On the wall of May there is a word trembling."

The History of the Round Window

The shadow that came in secretly through the round window facing north is, there's no mistaking it, his. (As far as I can tell from the shadow, he hasn't changed a bit since then.) Pulling a dream or laying himself upon himself was his habit, and coming in only with his "shadow" is just like him. But, even so, I marvel he remembered the round window at the back.

You may say it's an odd preconception, but anyhow, I can't face and talk to a shadow, so I first close the papered screen on the round window to convey my will. That is, the understandable thought that now he has appeared, I'd like him to keep me and this room (which, too, are supposed not to have changed a bit) company. The shadow stays in one corner of the faintly dark room by sectioning it off even more darkly, thereby probably indicating literally the entire amount of his thought that shut off that much light. (He hasn't changed.) I go around the room and turn off the ceiling lights one after another. The shadow gradually melts into the darkness of the wall; though, even then, it tries to maintain its outlines, barely, with a certain kind of darkness, but when I finish turning off the last light and turn to look, I can no longer recognize it anywhere. Now, only the round window retains the faint outside lightness.

And so, I robbed his shadow and forced it to keep my darkness company; but that may mean I was trapped into his design. By the time the silver-gray morning light gets into the room, the shadow will find itself laid upon my shadow. I'll have to admit that from the shadow showing double darkness. Despite myself I confront the circular brightness of the window. That must be the direction of his memory, as well as the moment it acquires itself in me. That is, him, in whom I confront him and who has hid himself in me.

The Stairs of the Bar

There's an amusing man who tripped on the stairs of a bar and sustained an external injury of the spirit. The wound's taking too long to heal, so sooner or later he'll go back to his wife's rural family, somebody said, but I wonder about that. If the staircase of the bar leads to the dark barn in the countryside, that's even more amusing. Outside the barn is an old well, as usual, and next to it, an impeccable stone lantern, and the silhouette of a tower in a rocket base, a silver plume rises, up in the sky the blue earth and the yellow moon, and now the one who's tumbled out the doors of the barn and risen to his feet is a large astronaut, that is, the amusing man who sustained the external spiritual injury. He doesn't even put on a helmet as he walks to the main house. The thing is not to go to the Ginza any longer. "Even if I get beaten," that bar hostess said at the top of the stairs, didn't she? "I'll never fall to my knees."

Genes' Pants

The afternoon left, the afternoon was born, and base mankind that is the vehicle of genes, still in its trousers, listened. The fingers were the vehicle's peripherals. There are several other peripherals, but is what's called self-consciousness lodged in them as well? If self-consciousness is to be confirmed by what's called laughter, ours unmistakably exists randomly in the route from fingers to mouth. The fingers grope for equipped signs and endlessly give birth to laughter. Spreading the five fingers, folding them like an umbrella, and stating the impression, "Like a chrysanthemum, like Mount Fuji," at the dwarfed spectacle, it was certainly funny. Two specimens of mankind once tried what's called arm-wrestling, making the feeble legs of a round table squeak, but meantime the afternoon was born, the afternoon left, and I could hear without interruption the baseball cheers of boys in the plaza from the open window. Even in the midst of arm-wrestling, we had the presence of mind to mutter, "Those, too, are the voices of multiplying genes, aren't they?" But then what the two specimens of mankind did! One, a lightning move involving pants. Two, imitation of frogs and such. Among others the interruption of self-consciousness about to form (somewhere over there a garbage can fell), the victory of the olfactory sense, and so on.

When I Looked Up, Only the Air

When I looked up, only the air around the anemometer atop the tower on the roof was faintly bright. My hands both flew to it and flaunted darkly. In the building which I had just come out of, the final reversal had occurred last night. As many walls as possible were taken away, so in the dance studio that was left, toward daybreak, several shrimp as thin as slides were now passing by. The building's structure that was a three-year paradox, regain your original shape. (After all, you are only me. "You," take off your dance shoes.) Both the hands of the person who had come out ahead of me and those of the people who came out with me have gathered around the rooftop anemometer. In the vague brightness, many a hand is flaunting, darkly.

Afternoon Offerings

Afternoon offerings, afternoon dreams. Afternoon impotence is defined for those pointed breasts slowly walking along the moat. Lukewarm fruits are more abstract than epistles and diaries and are therefore more appropriate for the definition of curses. But the ultimate art of "switching" does sometimes occur there. In the narrow room the historians whisper: "No fatigue yet?" "No offerings yet?"

Breasts pointed, you wash the lukewarm fruits in a corner of the room. Afternoon impotence is defined far more abstractly than in the personal notes; it's water, it's breath. The ultimate art of "lived evil." "Yes, in short, time is a palindrome." "It reads the same forward and backward."

Black stars that float up in the width of fingers and still follow the breath. In the room the water and the historians. You bend down, and semitones leak between your legs; you move your hands to them and switch them. —Cappello's floor, watery knees.

Afternoon offerings, afternoon dreams. Slowly descending to the low water, from which way was your palindrome read? From breasts, or from fruit? "Madam, I'm Adam. Or the reverse will be fine with me, too."

The Wool Palace

When the sun goes down, I'm told, "The ewe has such a pretty look in her eyes." Before collapsing on its own, it must show its outlines at least once: the Wool Palace. That I've come into town doesn't mean I can definitely come across them, but I look for the tower with a pretty look in its eyes. The evening dusk that's been cut off. Fragile battle in a private edition. Avoiding even that, I turn at a crossroads, and unyielding young women are keeping their upper bodies firm. "That's the symptom, and they are, unlike their appearances, as soft as fruit." The one who's whispered that into my ear, is he "the compassionate father"? But he also tells me, "Beyond that there's statue-like time, in which not even conversation is needed." Also, a sigh that has nothing to do with me: "In this town an unglazed salesman was a job that wasn't worth the pay." Or, a guide: "For the corny melancholy of the bustle on a bridge in the evening, turn here."

That invisible torii once sat astride someone's neck, I'm told. (*Shit!*) "Male midwife Ezra" who turned wool into a coat, and into a blanket as well, is going to be buried on the other side of the river, but this being the third-stage twilight, I can't even see that. (*Cluck!*) Well, what can I do? It was perhaps too late to come across the pretty look in her eyes. But immediately at my ear needless advice: "The preparations for awkward sleep are beginning." "No. Mankind's sleep."

Economical Silhouettes

There certainly were some who loved the economics of silhouettes, but they were unhappy. They, that is, those who could not recognize the sea of *gestes*, were always confused on the streets. They could not enter a restaurant which was managed as a hobby. Also, I assume they could not grasp the meaning of the staircase going down to the subway or the mercury lamp about to fade. Once in a while I saw them in an old restaurant, but they had their eyes closed, probably not to be confused any further. Everything should have been reduced to outlines for them. In other words, they could understand only borderlines; for the rest, the field of unpredictability kept expanding. Of course, even with silhouettes, a person can be a person, a flower can be a flower. Reductionists know that only omissions can be clear. But, unfortunately, for them it was: "Dog, a devil deified, deified lived a god." (This palindrome corresponds to their hidden hobby in reaction to expedient conformance.) They hated coincidences and, therefore unable to touch either "meaning" or "meaninglessness," were always confused on the streets.

No *geste* has tried to be an outline. They are always a sea. Be it morning, or be it night. And a *geste's* abrupt running-aground is a rock of calligraphy. If so, happy wrecked ship, read its "meaning" or "meaninglessness." Even more so, if it's the name of the old restaurant: —*"Mouquin," "Voisin," "Pré Catalan."*

The Nickname Is Armadillo

Two contracts: the original and a copy. Written in one: "Broken road," in the other: "Armored car" (the nickname: Armadillo). Am I to roll about on that floor, this floor? Contradiction in terms called perpetual fact. "You are happy because you don't have a past to which you can return in a shortcut sort of way; the reason for happiness of all kinds is that the past is cut off." The tall editor who, saying that, climbed the steep stairs in felt slippers, I hear, often hangs from a chinning device made of iron pipes, legs dangling, in the evening. This is the ultimate contradiction in terms. That in the hallway on the second floor he didn't even turn to look when he quickly added the following may suggest he'd made up his mind in some way: "Rolling on the floor is dated. That's a shame to gymnastics." And about to talk about personal things, in the short distance to his desk, he fluttered beige paper. I don't think he had much to boast to me. The road visible from the window was all broken. If the content was subsidiary, there was no need for a contract. But he nonetheless said: "Armadillo." —"My wife is a dentist. Her nickname is Armadillo."

A Canal Full of *Canaries*

Written on the plaster wall was *canary*, canal. *Hornbill*, horny. *Crow*, eat crow, too spicy. *Pheasant*, peasant. Turning around the wall, I met a peasant in a spice-colored coat. By some misunderstanding, he was carrying a narrow canal. Modernism is now over, ended just now, in fact, the peasant said. It was an age, you know, when *delicate* men like me could do things. "Don't you regret it?" I asked. To some extent, I wanted to be polite to a victim. "No, I'm rather grateful." "Are you sure?" "Yes. I don't have to do odd things any more. I have a canal full of *canaries*."

Peasant, *pheasant*. Too spicy to eat *crow*. Horny *hornbill*. Canal full of *canaries*. I turned to look at the silly road. Be polite. The canal, just as I had expected, had a spice-colored surface and created misunderstandings for the narrow-mindedness called modernism. But I pretended not to notice. A plaster wall, I said, but it was dirty. So much so that I'd hesitate to turn around it once again. But I was pretending not to notice. —"Over, or not over, either is fine. Isn't it?"

Even That Humming
(excerpts)

The Absolute Beginner

It was a songless morning. The legislators were hurrying "beyond that." You locked your small apartment. Collapsing wealth held in your arms, you were about to cross the Seven Seas. If youth for you has long been a thing of the remote past, there's nothing more to explain. Standing at a street corner where you can't turn right, you can only turn your eyes to the huge sign everyone shares. When the harbor is distant, the legislators will call it "land." But in a songless morning, a harbor for you alone appears. "Once again," you say. "Once again, I'll be the beginner."

Innumerable queries are repeated today as well. The huge sign tells of the remote past "beyond that." The town where you can't turn right can't always escape the land. But there are days when the legislators' "fraudulent stare" can't dominate. You, the absolute beginner. The one to cross the Seven Seas with collapsing wealth held in your arms. The harbor for you alone on a songless morning. "I have nothing to inherit," you say. "Overturn your dream of territory, like the insomniac Ulysses."

Lynne, Calm Morning

Avoid a shortage of explanations. Meet Lynne. Vending machine under the eaves. Pale territory of a mercury lamp. Loosened perspective. Late at night there's a shortage of spectacles. It is a pleasant sensation—.

Lynne. A perpendicular called Lynne. A calm miracle in a shortage of spectacles. I explained: Like a politician who's supported by an approval rate of 5 percent; about a window that the wind traveling the plaza reaches without adjectives; a black bird that drops diagonally outside the open door; distant thunder that guarantees that nothing happens. Lynne, Lynne in a shortage of spectacles, I had explained. . . .

Night clouds are in a single spot, and they remain on the rail until daybreak. Even on mornings when lines appeared in the plaza, she was concerned about the clouds. Where are those clouds, Lynne said. I couldn't find them from the window, but it was still a miraculously calm morning. There was a pigeon's voice, but it soon stopped. Lynne on a calm morning who doesn't leave her place, who is in a shortage of spectacles. Surely the clouds are insufficient, that's because, Lynne, I explained: That's because of the invisible wind blowing in the sky. Lynne, because of you, an invisible wind is blowing in the sky. . . .

Even That Humming

Pleasantly you walk on. Along the ditch in which an abstract loincloth flows as an eternal myth, pleasantly you are walking. The eternal wrinkle will have to be chiseled into your brow. The crows above the cultivated land, having abandoned their amity with the landscape, will be dancing feather-light above the silly ditch. Non-criticism on the periphery is always like this. Acceptance lacking immunity is thus a return to a clime in which even smiles stiffen.

Suppose one of the pitiable congregation, serious wrinkles lodged on his brow and trembling with a kind of sense of responsibility, has shown up in front of the entrance to a high-class Japanese restaurant. A talk on the myth from then on. In the earthen foyer he recited "The Wound of the West" and as expected it worked out as "Open, Sesame!" So, he, a bird in loincloth, ducked through the foyer, with a drawn bamboo sword, kicked at the legs of the waitress he bumped into first, overturned an arrangement of Zen food, blocked the line of trays in the hall, and delivered "The Wound" to the dining room (or thought he did). The border where black emotions, crow emotions, linger. *Dren-dre-dren.* But what is it that you truly long for? Wasn't the tune to which you danced in that *costume*, humming *Taan, La-la-la-la-laan,* after sweeping down the heavy screen doors, papered doors, wasn't that an intoxication you could have only on the periphery of the Eurasian Continent?

Come New Year. With no messenger from the peninsula, peaceful time appears to return. You may have to mutter to yourself, That talk wasn't too good. It was like gossip over tea between a crow and a loincloth, etc. —So, after all, you walk on pleasantly. Along a ditch in which an abstract loincloth flows, you are walking pleasantly. Will the envoy of the times finally blend into the humming of the crows? In the event, call the humming the swan lake. Even the nasal song, the humming.

Autumn Debt

"Autumn scream like a Messerschmitt," said the gentle boy who came in on the subway at Shibuya. "I'm holding it in my arms as a debt. I'd like to go to a beautiful woman, whom I've never met, to return this autumn debt." But in his suburban house, a narrow hallway where he can't even run must be waiting for him. Even while engaged in a quiet conversation, the boy has no choice but to go back there as he always does. Your debt is too beautiful. You won't meet the woman, I'm sure, tomorrow, or the day after tomorrow. I have no right to give you advice, but you'll remain holding the autumn scream like a Messerschmitt in your arms forever. Back home, you squeeze through the hallway with stacks of books, turn on the light in the tiny dining room, and smile at the thin vase and green ashtray. A Messerschmitt, did you say? I've never seen one myself. In your hand holding the handstrap, the autumn is quietly squeaking. Yes, your debt is too beautiful.

A Yellow Interest

When the poet came to "The Yellow Modern Period" with an almost comical self-confidence, he may already have been late. He should have realized that from the troubled smiles of the people around him. He should have noticed them exchanging glances among themselves. "For a civilization that's patched together," he said, "we'll call out ghosts of the past and let them talk one after another." Was that a dream that was out of place? But sneering men, things begin exactly when they've ended. That is a political truth that only a latecomer knows. The modern period was born as a legacy. So the poet died twice. And he turned into a yellow interest with a pout, with a pout.

The Structure of the Eggplant

Goddamn! I had told you eggplant isn't a "color," hadn't I? Born between formalist and imagist, the eggplant must have gone through its own painful experiences. In the event, if you knowingly explain it as "structurally, the camouflage of a leisurely shrimp," I can't dismiss the matter as simple ignorance. To be sure, the eggplant has never had bones in its insides. But what about it? Because it doesn't have bones, it must camouflage itself with adornments—with that kind of shortcut thinking, how do you propose to understand the troubles the eggplant had to go through for so long? I'm too appalled for words is what I am. You all observe only the surfaces with the "good eyes" of which you are so proud and simply delight in describing them. And with that, you think you saw through the eggplant's inner mechanisms. You feel you've conferred corporate status upon it. Before you know it, you switch a vegetable to fish or shellfish. Listen, fellows, despite its appearance, the eggplant is an individualistic vegetable. Each of them has its own "good history." If a vegetable were no more than a "color" or a "form," as you say it is, Tokyo Tower would be a carrot, Rokuharamitsuji Temple a tomato. If you brandish the myth of the eye and say everyone's the same, goddamn, you might as well destroy me with straw arrows and lotus guns!

The Pumpkin's Gallstone

Well, I suppose many of you won't believe this, but the pumpkin had a gallstone. The surgery was a success, so you should be relieved, but it's a mystery how the pumpkin developed a gallstone. There are many things you can't explain about human life, and this goes to show the pumpkin's life is similar. Surrounded by philistines, he (or she?) nonetheless grew up healthy. I don't imagine something like a gallstone would affect him too much, but anyhow he experienced surgery like *mankind*. From his sickroom the setting sun was beautiful, and it was just about that time that everyone came to see him. On his bed, half of him bathed in the sun, his normally wrinkled body deepened its shadows, as though his moderate personality had added some weightiness. "The stone's right here," he'd say. "Looks like a mushroom, doesn't it?" Those who came to see him were relieved by these accommodating words. But some fools would respond unthinkingly, "A mushroom in a pumpkin, you say?" This would make him frown suddenly. "I don't understand that myself. Seems contrary to the promise made at birth," he'd mutter, and clam up. "Well, you know, *mankind*, too, has a mushroom type of gallstone," someone would try to soothe him, but too late. It was the silence of the stern pumpkin staring at the huge setting sun. The visitors who happened to be in that spectacle all felt solemn, or so they said. In fact, it couldn't have been something that touched a taboo, but I wouldn't second-guess.

Looking at a pumpkin's gallstone and the beautiful setting sun, anyone would become somewhat philosophical.

Madame Cucumber

I live in a field where Madame Cucumber is. Whatever happened to that wish? I say as though it were somebody else's business; I am that casual. By way of sauntering idly, I took a look at the patch and I got hold of something long, but it, too, was a well-made Madame Cucumber. Ample and compassionate Madame Cucumber who, they say, willingly thrust herself into an anus during a certain age. Her coloration of course, but her figure is also splendid. Because one side of me likes to work and dislikes jokes, I think positively of such harvests of walks. If I don't pay attention, regardless of the Alpha and Omega past, I even try to learn the art of making it in the world. When it comes to intentions, it's Madame Cucumber. When it comes to desires, too, it's Madame Cucumber. Because settlements of history are that free and easy, I, though serious, can survive in this field, just idling away. Be that as it may, Madame has recently written in her personal notes: "I recognize that my good figure was of no use after all. It pains me somewhat to say this at my age, but I also failed in putting a lid on the uneasy period. But please do forget personal things for me. From now on I'll pamper you as best I can."

The Bad Taste

Shall I sing *Tan, tan, tan*? At the edge of a black field, looking at a black stand of trees and a black stream, shall I sing *Tan, tan, tan*?

If you say there's still time till morning, I'll stomp around a black house, trample on its modest flower garden, and bring back a half-hearted chaos to this "licentious plain" in this time frame without proverbs.

In the box in the big sky a shrimp captures a smelt, and in the water box two rats mate. My room still cold, I do nothing but make a noise of bad taste. To be barbarous, you need to think only a bit. Children who come home late at night. Spending two hours on a five-minute distance. That's because they too trample on the black night without proverbs. Shall I sing *Tan, tan, tan*?

Still, I have a man ahead of me. He's a philistine in a polka-dot shirt who, scratching his neck with empty eyes, hurt the interior decorator psychologically. He still owns a coal stove. Here's also a pseudo-sage who performs the ancient times in a country under a mercury lamp where "ugly flowers" bloom luxuriously. These are the people who in childhood threatened their parents by brandishing a protractor.

This late at night I chase unhappy animals around and overturn someone's dream. And I dive into a bed with many stones, so that, surrounded with "unprecedented luxury," my body returns to the medieval ages. That's my scheme. Well,

that's the extent of my barbarity, shall I sing *Tan, tan, tan?*
This late at night without proverbs, while trembling for lack of
any measure to go by, shall I sing *Tan, tan, tan?*

Until the Water of the Fountain Runs Dry

Now, a dark cloud is dancing around the fountain. I don't have to lie about it. It is a figure of my "conflict." I see a leg of the light plunging deep into it from the sky above, but that's for a second, and there's no hint of the "conflict" ending. I hear that there's a fellow who goes about expounding unnecessarily that the self is in danger of collapsing. That's silly, and also dishonest, talk. In the end, that's no different from those who advise, Be conscious of the other in thyself. I, as an observer of fountains with the right pedigree, have followed unalloyed history, but the "conflict" has always been an external manifestation. "Thou," too, is no more than a concrete example of the other that's updated.

The dark cloud dancing around the fountain has suddenly increased in volume, threatening to swallow the dichotomous (in reality, friendly) flat schema. The light in the sky above still exists, but that's history sought in a different order and can't participate in the present disturbance. Renew your life! Renew your life! Make it still newer, still newer. Different footnote, special footnote, history of the weak, the crisis of the chameleon-like self. Don't turn your eyes to such a charitable context, which is trivialized each time it's repeated. Yes, I am a shamelessly independent-minded, unalloyed observer. Dance, dark cloud, ghoulishly. Until the water of the fountain runs dry.

The Artificial Leg and the Parfait

I'd like to have reason enough to say that I have nothing to do with it no matter how beautiful hours visit me. The man with an artificial leg who said he didn't like anything soft wrote letters all day at the round table on the terrace. At dusk he mailed the letters which he (must have) crammed with minute handwriting in front of the station building. The outlines of the two-story, three-story buildings near the station were sharp, as well as fierce. The "philosophical" sky slow to darken was deep and blue. If the incident in early summer is something like that, if it is no more than that, —I wouldn't have felt ashamed to assert I "had nothing to do with it." The one-legged man had a pair of light-green sunglasses on the thin bridge of his nose and danced a small dance for me under cherry trees lining the street, lest he fall into the trap of perspective. The story was, he was loved by many as the youngest member of the Veterans Association of Western Australia.

Because at age twenty-two I lost what was beneath my knee that was treated too late, I hate soft things. He approached me with these words when, sitting at the round table next to his, I had just ordered a red parfait "Angel's Bottom" after a great deal of hesitation. I welcomed with a corny smile the allegorical form loading a large glass plate and destroyed it with the tip of my spoon. An artificial leg and a parfait. —"Is there any relationship between them?" He gently shook his head and returned his eyes to his letter pad. One letter is addressed to me, and it will be delivered to my round table at a "certain time" in my life. I imagine its opening, for example, as follows: "In a tent without a doctor, I was fed only soft things. To prevent me from masticating 'forms' of slight fever, perhaps."

If Bowlegged, You Are in the Writing Business

That autumn day, the bowlegged man appeared. The receptionist gave me the message, "Bowman," but it was probably not so much humor as a symptom of an emotion. It is a receptionist's fate to be always exposed to amorphous malice in the budding state. There was also a whispered comment, "He's a typhoon in the foyer, sir." But when I took a look, he was just a gentle, big man. He had his enormous, long upper body bent over the round table that was part of the reception set, sharpening a pencil expertly. Dropping fragrant shavings into a marble ashtray. We looked at each other and rose to our feet, and my eyes were forced to take a perfectly ascending vertical angle. Also, taking a descending vertical angle, I confirmed his famed bowlegs through which a soccer ball was said to easily pass. But what in fact passed through it was a couple of lobsters that were the crystallizations of the hall. Picking up one of them, I looked for my own emotion that would be appropriate for a conversation at an ascending vertical angle.

"Please correct it as soon as you can," the man said. Though he did so in a gentle tone. "Everything has changed for me." "Must be only *your* circumstances." I handed him the lobster. It at once turned into a pencil and, in the hands of the man who seated himself again, was sharpened expertly, fragrantly. I told the woman receptionist, "Dive." Firming up her emotions and turning her upper body first into a lobster, she dove between his bowlegs. It seems she will also be sharpened expertly. "My circumstances require a most up-to-date title." "I understand. If bowlegged, you are in the writing business."

The Green Theater

The theater where a green lamp sways in the wind doesn't even reveal the number of its actors, and it often provokes angry voices from people who do not try to understand the situation. It seldom announces the names of the plays. You can see why when you learn that the theater is known for its unpleasant setup in which half the audience is put on the stage, half forced down to the orchestra seats, spending concocted awkward hours every time. The trained actors hide among them and, as soon as the awkwardness begins to go away, cut apart the stage and orchestra again with a skillful yell deceptive of the age.

That bald, short-legged man came to visit the theater on a quiet evening. "I'd like to buy two tickets. I am two persons." The old actor who was in the foyer didn't flinch but asked, "May I ask which age you are from?" "Despite the way I look," the man replied, putting his hand on his red head, "I was born only recently." "Well, how about the other you?" "Forty-four years old, bald, and short-legged. I think you know about that very well." "I see. But only one of you can get in. Whichever one will be all right, though." But the man abruptly swung the actor aside with a force you wouldn't have expected from his body. The actor, too, wasn't deterred, and he flung a well-trained voice at the back of the man who was dashing toward the theater. "Wait, you! The two of you won't do. One of you to the stage, the other to the orchestra!"

Anti-Cherry-Blossom Man

Cherry blossoms are everywhere. The sculptor who hurt his mouth on a stone meal offered late at night was a cherry-blossom man; so was the small old man who had his legs planted in a slowly tilting cast stove to hold it steady. The remote relative who lost sight of his "category of interest" by the lake on a balmy spring day. The guitarist who once stepped on a medieval screen painting and made a hole in it. In other words, all those who prepare for tomorrow with a vulnerable heart are cherry-blossom men. Yesterday I saw cherry-blossom men piled high like bestsellers being shipped out. It was a song-less, quiet sight only possible in peaceful times. Their wounds faintly red, they must be dancing in a wind on some street corner. But I don't annotate them. I am an anti-cherry-blossom man, even though I repeat half-hearted greetings everywhere!

Spring Mirror   *for Kitatsuji Yoshihisa*

We are militarily handsome men. If it's a mirror of the cherry-blooming time, you can see it. "The horse carriage stolen from a Chinaman" was buried in the sand of dream, but to flow over it right and left like students is a sweet-smelling military affair only possible for handsome men. We begin our assessment. "In a certain period in China I understand the word percussion instrument flew. From the mirror I can see in that direction the wounds of the West and the eyebrows of the East in the distance." "No, wait. Take off our spring shirts, and we may still be flowing like those students." "Militarily, doesn't that also mean men who were handsome in the past?"

The Rainbow

What we were most proud of were the baskets our tribe made. Come weekend dusk, a man in a white uniform stood at the crossroads and with a hand flag directed the baskets that kept coming from the four directions. The baskets, which are properly twisted, which look larger the farther you move away from them, and which on the whole are pregnant with deep transparency even with a faint suggestion of a rainbow in the four corners, are prized as exceptional. The baskets of my tribe were impeccable in every one of those respects. Whenever we showed up with our baskets at the crossroads in the evening darkness, the man in the white uniform would always raise his hand flag high with a blissful expression. "Oh, these are the ideal. They are the baskets among baskets, which go far beyond the dreams of the village," he would whisper to my uncle or aunt. Our divine products would be loaded on the truck at the very end, which would then envelope the deck with soft rainbow colors, eliciting sighs from the surrounding people. Those seeing the truck off would remain voiceless, clustering close together, as they kept watching our baskets which became larger as they receded, the baskets which, near the pass, moved along the rim of the hill like semi-transparent mists.

Thus, every weekend, our tribe's baskets were lost beyond the pass, probably without any meaning whatsoever. To seal my discontent, my father, who was still young, would tell me, "It's good that they're appreciated. However, our only pride lies in not tiring of weaving them." But I always shook my head. Was he saying tradition was no more than a rainbow spanning the four corners? Because I was young I was immersed in the dreams of the village and could not at all understand a thought like his. Being uncompensated is so beautiful, but wasn't it, by any chance, to compensate for the suspicion our prideful tribe could not bring itself to state clearly? Yes, to make an honest confession, I still can't wipe away the sense of not understanding it completely.

The Ships and the Snow

To look at "the ships and the snow," she went up to the window on her three coarse legs. Because I, who say this, was also being forced to be an odd number emotionally, I ostentatiously threatened her as she turned her back, saying, "I can't stand any of your caresses."

Outside the window beautiful "yellow-green monks" had formed a circle. Their chests, from which steam rose, were to indicate the direction in which they were to move without breaking up the circle, that is, the solution of "the ships and the snow," or "the silent silhouette" of "the ships and the snow."

In the end, I succumbed to the cold of the afternoon without caresses and, without getting up, spent amorphous time in the blanket trying to make some coherence out of the numbers. She (whom I "threatened" as she turned) was—how many before her? I made several errors and I was also appalled by my unreliable memory, but an odd number seemed natural after all.

It was an afternoon when the sound of the snow melting continued endlessly. I closed my eyes, and that yellow-green circle had already left the plaza and was taking a stone-paved road to approach a forest of masts. Breakdowns tend to come to us abruptly. "Let's look at the ships and the snow," I finally said. "Los Olvidados, let's form a circle." Then, outside the window, slight quakes occurred. Lumps of snow had fallen one after another from the leaves of the hemp palm (from their sacerdotal robes). "It's too late. Besides, that number is wrong, too."

The Patrick Century
(excerpts)

One Who Never Sleeps Deeply

Catnap. It was an incomparably beautiful word to me once upon a time. There must be someone on this earth who never sleeps deeply. He's always on the alert, waiting. This beautiful word was born for him. . . . Catnap in an attic in a remote town assaulted by a midnight rain. Or catnap in a seashore shack at dawn with low oppressive clouds. He's having shallow sleep, his thick chest wrapped in a coarse green blanket. Imagining such a man often brought peace to me, a boy who spent sleepless nights. The man surely is a terrorist, and in the morning a coup d'état will start. Though it's still dark, he will rise to his feet without even yawning, peer out of a gap in the louver door, and walk out onto the wet asphalt road, a heavy canvas bag on his shoulder. Like an alert animal, he will choose his path among the back alleys before disappearing into a stone building where a couple of his comrades wait. I smile for that terrorist. One who never sleeps deeply, my blanket isn't green, but like you I will close my eyes for a catnap. Until morning when a coup d'état starts, I, too, will have shallow sleep like an animal.

Of course, the morning I had was always one without a coup d'état. I might copy a terrorist every night, but not a single armored vehicle appeared in the morning. Rubbing my eyes for lack of sleep, I would go down to the dining room where I would spread the newspaper on the round table merely to confirm the beginning of an utterly eventless day. Before long, the imaginings of my boyish days receded into the distance, and my insomnia gradually faded. But even now, when I hear the word catnap, the feel of the blanket, that green blanket which I in real life never held in my hands, gently revives in me. You who never sleep deeply, I have left you behind on the earth in my distant memory, but I have not forgotten the beautiful sound of the word. The midnight order, still in force, must be making the terrorist with a thick chest steal a catnap in a small room a quarter century away. This is why I feel a faint disappointment each time I wake up in the morning without a coup d'état and look through the gap between the curtains down on the street without any armored vehicle. Stay on the alert, I whisper to myself. Stay on the alert, not sleeping deeply, though the times may be peaceful. Yes, that word is incomparably beautiful even now.

The Fish in Idaho

The young black woman was frying American fish in her small kitchen. There was a sizzling sound of oil for quite some time. Eating fish for breakfast was totally foreign to me. In time she came out carrying a loud, large yellow plate with two fish on it. The plate was placed in the middle of the tablecloth with a crab design, and the two of us sat at the table, face to face. Her polished dark skin. If she turns her young eyes to me, I'll have no choice but to eat some of the two gray fish. So thinking in my muddy head, I looked out the window at the dry plain. The fish were too big for my hangover stomach, and the sticky smell of the spices covering them withered my appetite. With the window at her back, she appeared very slender. Against the backlight, she moved a knife and fork with her shapely hands and put some of the flesh she loosened on my small plate.

This is a dry place without a lake or a river. Where did they catch these fish? I asked the young woman against the backlight. "Underground fish," she replied. I did not understand well what she meant, but I carried to my mouth a piece of underground flesh that had turned light-green with olive oil. It had an unexpectedly plain taste. Whatever it may be, it has to be a freshwater fish. "I went out and bought them while you were asleep. Just as all the women in your home country do."

Do you always eat underground fish in the morning? I asked. "If you want to, you can do that," she muttered, looking out at the desert. She must have misunderstood the meaning of my words. She turned her eyes away; I had not known anything as beautiful as her profile. "I wouldn't mind it every morning," she laughed a little. "Catching fish is a lot of work." Tablecloth with a crab design. Late morning light. Her slender hands took some flesh for me again. "I wonder if fish in Idaho know how to go down the stairs."

Book of Paintings: The Setting Sun

"Ouch!" there was someone's voice. It came from the other side of the bookcase. The book my "unconsciousness" threw out seemed to have hit the famous skeptic, Ms. O. Because it was a terribly heavy book of paintings, it might have created a wound on her head requiring a couple of stitches. For a while there was an exchange of silences, before, as expected, she threw the book back toward me. My eyes followed its arrogant trajectory. The gigantic book slowly went over the bookcase, began to add to its volume as it descended, and attacked a wooden desk, swirling up an improbable amount of powder and dust. Of course, the work surface was smashed at once. What a terrible woman, was the unreasonable impression I had. She almost squashed me. But. It was none other than me that realized a serious cognitive error a few seconds later. The relationship between reality and consciousness is difficult, but at times the latter swallows up the former. That is, what had stabbed into the desk before my eyes was Ms. O's consciousness "swirling up powder and dust." Behind the bookcase the consciousness had annexed the book; only then, the consciousness so amplified had depicted the threatening parabola. My "unreliable" unconsciousness tried to escape. Regretting, I shouldn't have thrown the book; that was so light-headed. But the embarrassing thing was that the reality of my legs didn't make a well-coordinated move. My unconsciousness was caught up with by Ms. O's consciousness just before the door and faced its final moments. When you think of it, the title of the book was unfortunate: *Surrealists: The Setting Sun*. Naturally for a skeptic, Ms. O had long argued that solid surreality should not be tied to "unreliable" unconsciousness. She was angry that the linkage was the sort of thing only enfeebled men think up. She was born to possess a consciousness "inured to powder and dust." And she was secretly waiting for an opportunity to amplify the volume of her consciousness.

I had created an unexpected situation, but such things happen in life. I thought about it and went behind the bookcase to check Ms. O's wound. It appeared that the book hadn't hit her right on the head. On the contrary, when I looked at her face, I saw a graceful smile. Au-huh, she hadn't even sustained a scratch. She'd spectacularly duped me. "Ouch!" I growled, despite myself. "Damn you!" "Aha! O, ho! You now have got it, right? Surrealism is the powder and dust that consciousness swirls up, you see."

Goddamn God Dog

Today, from this moment on, every god will be called a dog. That Age of the Yellow Wind when every god had to be called a god in order to prevent the deities' intervention was a mere philosophical accident. Even now, the past, pregnant with alarming contingency, is waiting for our misunderstandings, but in order not to fall into that trap, too, we must call a god a dog, a top a pot, leg gel.

Goddamn god dog. Let me give an immediate example. One of those with pseudonyms, at his imperturbable age, has moved to a suburban town that looks like a stage set. The best part of it is it's close to the station, he says. That's the extent of my great determination, but that's "not much of" a reason to be made light of! he feigns self-mockery, but that is his infant skill to avoid a philosophical accident. Thus, on holidays, the man in my example unhurriedly looks down upon the enviable garden of his neighbor. On the sunlit lawn "the trap of a spectacle" of grandchildren running about occurs, so that, to get rid of the "misunderstanding," a god dog waiting for food with his large mouth open is called for on the peaceful lawn.

But, to be honest, the fate of the god's dog is fragile. It is no more than an accident of nouns that men who have reached the imperturbable age encounter just about when the memories of yellow winds have become unreliable. But, you, sages, that, too, is all right, isn't it? Today, from this moment on, call every god a dog with great determination. Tar the rat, and turn your leg into gel. An accident you may call it, but if it's nouns such as these, that's "not much of" a reason to be made light of. In an attempt to make some sense out of all this, let me install here a palindrome of "a similar degree": "God lived as a devil dog."

The Ducks and Advice

The small duck looks at Susan. The big duck doesn't look at Susan. Such contradictions better be disposed of soon. That's because the powers to look at "light" aren't equal. As Susan crouched, the light on the surface moved. The reason she crouched was to scoop the water. The big duck was floating near the other end of the pond. You couldn't tell whether it was male or female. I've long had this question: Why are male and female similarly shaped? When you start thinking of its reasons, every one of them turns out to be a cliché. As the secular world holds it, the male is a potential father, but its position is no more than a moral born of "a non-existent daughter," the reverse of a tabooed emotion, as it were. That biological hypocrisy has prevented a situation where, for example, the male could be a bird and the female, a fish. This is not the sort of story to be transmitted in secrecy.

Anyway, the big duck has to be male according to an ordinary conjecture, and its looking at Susan has to be iconographically correct. The small duck is in the shadow of a shrub, his beak turned toward the "light." Still, big and small may be created by the relations of distances, and there's the possibility that male and female may be reversed. I'm already laughing. This is because all things are light and, in that case, contradictions may lie in the inequality of light. Looking at light is a misunderstanding. Light can't possibly "be looked at." So. The question goes back to the starting point. The light on the surface of Susan scooping the water moved. When she crouched, unequal powers emerged. At that moment, was Susan the name of a blank? Were the ducks, big and small, born as a misunderstanding of that? Or was Susan the impossible father of herself?

Elegia Moderna   *in the margins of Kitatsuji Yoshihisa*

<Pot on a Tree>

The one looking for the pot on the peninsula was a large girl in a pullover dress. She looked up with narrowed eyes, once, at the pot bathed in the afternoon sun on a terebinth with scant branches at the cape, but she just passed by, her pull-over dress undulating. That youth who, during the cape night, put the pot on the tree surreptitiously may be a craftsman in the artless category of love. Let the peninsular pot float at an appropriate angle, and it turns into a myth on a tree of sorts. What was left after the "misunderstanding woman" walked off was, everyone must admit, an elegant structure called an ascending vertical angle.

But the category of love is solitary. You look at it again, and the pot in the sunshine begins to appear sunk in a brittle hermaphrodite dream at that height. An afternoon pot that floats at an elegant yet lonely ascending vertical angle. Yes, perhaps I should say it's a category of solitude on a tree destined not to catch the eyes of a girl, her pullover robe undulating.

<The Lamp and the Breeze>

One lonely ship must fade away in order to leave a single lamp on its "lost" bow. If the breeze that once caressed the Age of Monuments envelops the small porcelain plate of the lamp, will one of those who were with us turn into a statue and circulate a modest ancient dream? But what halts the statue about to walk must also be the breeze that has traveled across the past. "Doubt today's light, and that is the lost leading edge of loneliness."

<Spears of Songs>
The night insomniac warriors play
Spears of banners, spears of walls
Spears of songs oblivious of military exploits

<Devotion>
The student's pot, once ensconced in an iron box, was the lady's pot. Asked for this ludicrous devotion, he didn't even scream because he was given a golden dream in the sealed darkness. "Let's not tell the others," he said. "I'll be happy only if the secret of our pot is kept." Outside the box, the lady smiled gently. But the student had no way of knowing—that hers was a smile directed to "others."

<The Hand-Mirror's Path>
The hand-mirror is a path to gray monks. The "woman of distinguished lineage" toys with the path like a religious painting.

One young man had grown fiercely thin because he lived behind the bronze hand-mirror. It was the startling emaciation of his torso which countervailed the immediate light and the bronze darkness. Will it emerge or fade away? The hand-mirror after all is a vessel of unsettling ideas and its shape is always within hesitations "Cancel, cancel it, if it isn't too late," he heard "her slip of the tongue." Or was it a secret seduction? The words also toyed with him like a feeble monk.

If we trace the figure's hesitations further, will we be on an escape journey oblivious of our status? Will we in time be wandering around the altar paintings somewhere near Urbino? But we won't ask for the details. The hand-mirror after all is a path to gray monks. We only know the emaciation like the religious painting of a torso toyed with by a slip of the tongue.

<The Curtain's Maxim>

The history of blue horses ended. The moment we swished the hems of the curtain together, unexpectedly it ended. It was a disappointing end of a fierce order. But we couldn't dance for joy. Because there was a maxim, which has been orally transmitted on this dark planet, that the curtain after strangulating a horse balloons in preparation for the advent of the next order—an amoral maxim, which, if interpreted, might turn into a disquieting convent.

It was, yes, in "that phase" that he appeared. From a distance he looked old, but he was young. The pedestal on which he stood had the curtain's *massive* folds, which are the nemesis of history, carved into it. A small bronze nude, which, if interpreted, rises on the strangulated blue horse. Its feeble-looking eyes tell of the disquiet of the amoral maxim. . . .

The planet will begin to talk about the next phase sooner or later. The unreliable youth will head for the fierce staircase.

We, who didn't dance for joy, saw that, too. A repeated maxim on a dark planet. Yes, the hems of the curtain on the planet were gathered for the fulfillment of the disquieting convent, and the history of blue horses ended too easily.

The Banquet of the Weathervane

It's the custom of this mansion to stop compiling laws on a day of a strong south wind and entertain with a new wine. Fill a deep bowl with olive branches entwining around it with a new wine, and the wise men, young and old, end up starting a gayeous banquet at once. The progress of the compilation of laws, which is the main thing, isn't too good, but that's to be expected: during the season of new wines, the south wind blows ferociously almost every day. Look, now: even the official who comes intending to urge hard work becomes swirled up by the momentum of the carousel, decides that the laws won't be finished for some time anyhow, and leaves, reeling through the town in the warm wind. It's about time to send a messenger for the publication—such worries belong only to the sober townsfolk. At the mansion these days, they are divining the direction of tomorrow's wind by erecting a ladle in the emptied deep bowl. That goes to show how self-indulgent the legislators are. Tell you what: the town where no messenger is likely to be sent, the town where the banquet of the weathervane continues—this isn't something I can tell the countries eagerly waiting for the laws, is it?

Bronze Marble

From the twilight port, I headed for an island floating in the Adriatic Sea, as a single aged statue, with a couple of other insomniac youths. The deck of the boat gradually darkened, and the whiteness of the waves in the wake alone was distinct behind us. Male and female forms began to blur. "Suppose I were a statue like a model of muscles," a silly young man who was beside me delivered a line to his group, obviously thinking he was being witty, "will it be bronze or marble?" "Yours is a human body bound to atrophy," a beautiful woman retorted, also obviously thinking she was being witty. "So is mine."

It would be very late at night by the time the boat arrived at the island. In any case, the handsome forms of these people would blend into the deep darkness over the sea, be they bronze or marble, or youths bound to atrophy or not. Far beyond the wake there was a low line of lights of the port. "What will you be, sir? Won't you fall apart?" an unexpectedly gentle voice asked me. The boat turned on the headlight. The surface of the sea rose up black. "How about it? Will you be an immortal statue?" Chin in hand on the railing, I closed my eyes. Yes, youths who can't sleep may fall apart. But in the Adriatic Sea I sleep well. . . .

Translations of the Sun

Translations of the sun! So that was this light of green! Standing in the afternoon studio, I hesitated a moment, and that turned into a feeling of surprise. That was an unexpected reason for the paintings to be green. But, come to think of it, when I turned on the narrow stone-paved road in the seaside town toward the painter's house, the corner was already enveloped in green haze. The light emanating from what appeared to be the window of the painter's room had softly dyed its surroundings. The painter opened the door with a gentle smile on his face and guided me to the source of the light. It was a large room you could not have expected from the plaster walls outside. Many a giant tableau stood around us, every one a landscape painting of a field. In every painting the horizon was high, with grassland nondescriptly spreading from the foreground. The sky left as a token was flesh-colored. There was nothing else. Things like trees, paths, and distant farmhouses weren't found in any of the tableaux. Only variations of green, with the foreground almost yellow-green that grew bluer into the distance, dominated the quiet canvases.

Truth was, I visited the painter at his house because several days earlier I had seen one of his tableaux in an exhibition and had been drawn to the deep quietude of the shifting green. As I looked at the large pieces lined up against the walls in his studio, I was seized by a wonderment: Why does he repeatedly paint such similar pictures? "Translations of the sun," muttered the painter after a long silence. Eyes turned to his paintings, he continued: "The sun doesn't change. So the canvases follow it." "But you have depicted only a field." "No, that isn't it," he said emphatically. As I flinched, he said accusingly, "These are not nature. These are translated light."

Seashore Logic

With a serious face you asked me about the type of logic that inhabits the seashore, pale kid brother. If I may answer now, I understand it as a dualism. After that the fruit on the table shattered. In the evening darkness the smell of a durian struck me powerfully. In a room with all its windows open, my lover was about to face a tropical night. I could say it was an odd yet beautiful triangular composition. The two windows facing the sea had the silhouettes of my brother and my lover. I drew two lines with my eyes. I was at their apex.

Late at night my brother left. Now, I can understand the meaning of your question. Why is it that this quiet triangle in the seashore cottage makes me as uneasy as a diagram on a hot night? Why is it that someone must give up? There was no sound of waves on the inland seashore, and the heavy wind that moved from time to time made the darkness of the durian breathe. The irrational militancy of our love after we let my brother go. The shattered tropical fruit.

My brother's motorboat circled the narrow dark bay twice with exploding noises and disappeared beyond the black cape. "Egoist," she pointed at me sunken in a rattan chair. That was a word I hadn't thought of, but as time passes, it's within the category of dualism. To be sure, the seashore logic may not be anything more than irrational running-around. But, brother, you who left shattering the dark surface of the water, now, I can answer you this way, too. However fierce, love can't, militarily, be exempt from running-aground.

Until I Hear the Heretic Voice

I turned at a crossroads. The wall ended at the canal. Water, teeth, voice, fragile things, I don't know what to do with adjectives until I hear the heretic voice.

*

Some say it is a strait of low sounds, others that it is a messenger of lowlands. As time rotates, a passion for such "lows" can be observed. Or grass of low efficiency, a walking stick of low humidity. The plywood house I visit is even lower. Consciousness will head for a descending vertical angle on its own. Until I hear the heretic voice.

*

I shouldn't mind it. I'm not a pitiful angel in a dream. Girls with white teeth and cheerful voices, who were paid to ride a "gondola" with small bills. In the meantime, the man who thought only of interests slept in a narrow patch of grass on the other shore. Sad feelings will remain, but that's all right, too; I can't become an angel.

*

A speaker's cracked voice. A distant round dance music riding the wind. At the crossroads there are "sounds" like that.

A dream begets a dream, and I peer into "the lowness," but where am I? Whose shadow am I? Water, teeth, voices. Ones sinking at a descending vertical angle. I don't stand awhile like an angel. Yes, the wall may end at the canal, until I hear the heretic voice.

Music on a Hot Morning

Acrobat from dream to dream, or merry-go-round. I wasn't told what was between them, but "the animal skin" we playfully wounded will fall "somewhere outside" tomorrow. That's our moral, or is it our anti-moral? Something that insignificant.

*

There is an "unwelcome" word: celebrity tax. The man who talked about it wasn't much of a celebrity. The water increased little by little, and yellow and green illuminations were wavering on its black surface. I think I'll say anything, whatever it may be, to the extent I understand it. Even about the meaningless discrimination between being a celebrity and not being, at a rainy midnight.

*

A hot morning when birds fly and heat haze rises from the streets. Humiliations since last night which are randomly distributed. I was told forgetting even that would be beneficial. "To be sure," you whispered. "To be sure, the memories that repeat themselves, come back to you time and again, are a pain, I'd say." As a matter of fact, in a room with no siblings, the emotions that surface are thin. Somewhere we'll have to set up a moment to "forgive." It is also necessary to make sure beforehand of the distance to the seashore, to the pantheon.

*

Gerrymander, enclosure, heavy smoker in Tokyo. That's about it, the extent of my understanding. Acrobat from dream to dream. Giants on the seashore who make thunderous noises. To put it another way (though I don't need to put it another way), it's the hot morning when *Jakuson* paid a celebrity tax. We all have an animal skin and will fall "somewhere outside" tomorrow. To put it another way, music on a hot morning, the pantheon you go to with a discount ticket if you are no celebrity whatsoever!

Vanished Flowers, Dreams and Sacrifices

To me, vanished flowers. To you, dreams and sacrifices. The afternoons are extremely simple. Therefore, you can even repeat them with ink and pen. To us in a small gray room, unfinished novel, and music.

*

But. Suppose there was a man as handsome as, for example, a movie star, who announces that unfinished is the beginning of an end! Sum up eccentricities from there, and we "can't get beaten by anybody." Like an old religious sect, or like a tall housemaid, we know, we know everything. What lies beyond that, further than that, and far beyond that: vanished flowers, dreams and sacrifices.

*

Saffron in the market. I rejected the sweet talk and selected a cheap one, and also selected beautiful wrapping paper. These old men who once carpeted the streets with flowers of various colors and held their eccentric weapons ready beyond them. That afternoon (when the bells began to ring in the midst of silence, they say) also, had it been announced that it would be unfinished? Was a picturesquely handsome man lying beside them? La Rambla of flowers. Late dreams on the peninsula.

When the sun sets, we turn into soft statues and go out for a walk. In a suburban town, blending into the imagined crowds. If we follow our dream, we may be able to carpet this town without bell towers with vanished flowers. But now, I'm not that old, nor a picturesquely handsome man, either. "That's yellow saffron." Yes, beyond that, and further beyond, to me, vanished flowers, to you, dreams and sacrifices.

Dream of a Circle

I will not hand my past to anyone. I won't, even if it sounds like a scream, or even if it's like a "muddy sea." In that shack late at night, I formed a phantom circle for you. I shouted with forgotten people. Out of the shack, the earth was muddy. The circle began to proceed in the rainy darkness. Our shouts at times sounded like a scream.

I will not hand my past to anyone. I won't, even if it's torn apart by days of hesitation, or even if it's creaking like the power of collapse. That circle late at night was a celebration executed for you. From the seaside shack to a muddy crossroads, from the crossroads to the dark wharf pushing back the muddy waves, we proceeded, shouting.

Were you waiting for me? Did our celebratory voice already reach you? Yes, if it's a dream, it can remain a dream. I will not hand my past to anyone. The past is a phantasmagoria that exists with forgotten people. A shout like a scream rises from the dream of a circle.

CARDIFF UNIVERSITY
PRIFYSGOL CAERDYDD

Kokaco-lar

There are many kinds of road. The snakes' road. The birds' road. The mosquitoes' road. And there's also the sadists' road.

I'm not much of a sadist, but if it's about that white road, I'm not loath to listen. It begins with a dream of a slave market outside the town (it's a Dutch-style old market), proceeds on a gray horse along a dusty road (the woman walking by me is the one I'd bid on), crosses a pebbly brook, and leads to an expansive mansion surrounded by a reddish brick fence. . . .

The woman in the dream was first taught to memorize two words: *It-hart* and *Fore-gib-mi*. Words whose meanings weren't to be understood. Empty words with which to count the "eternity" of each room.
Caressing the long table in the dining room, she said, "*Fore-gib-mi*." In the large room with the bamboo blinds pulled down, she muttered, "*It-hart*."
Then, each time she moved from room to room, she repeated: *It-hart, Fore-gib-mi*.

That, too, is a road. It still is a road of some kind. The day has turned white, the man whispered. "I was tired. Of that repetition."
A white day that never ends in an appropriate way.
In the empty dining room, its floor of bricks the same color as

the walls, I stuck a straw into the bottle of lukewarm Coca-Cola and looked around.

Where did the road start? In the market beyond the dust. What was the one who followed me by horse? The woman in a dream.

"Look at the bottle! The bottle! The bottle! I'll lift a bottle and show it to you."

Its brown sweet water. I lifted the bottle and whispered a toast to myself and sucked up the brown water with the straw.

That, too, is a road. A slow road, which has to follow "beginning-shift-finale" that tends to be interrupted. But the woman's outline suddenly begins to blur. The drowsiness that I haven't felt for long tries to prevent my vacant dream, me with Coca-Cola in one hand. . . . The poinsettia on the large table, the black cat in the dining room, the red sandals waver. Though the white day has just started, a fierce drowsiness is assaulting me. The blackened beams on the ceiling, the demons painted on glass, shelves carved out of wood begin to blur.

I hastily put the straw in my mouth and sucked up the sweet water of eternity.

"Look at the bottle! The bottle! The bottle!"

A wind from a distant mine is moving the curtain. I wander the watershed of drowsiness, reeling.

What the woman stretches her hand to touch first is a vulgar sandstone candlestick. Caressing the sculpture shaped like a rearing horse, she mutters, *It-hart.*

The wind from the mine balloons the curtain hugely. That moment, too, she says, *It-hart, Fore-gib-mi,* and smiles despite herself.

I wander the watershed. "As long as I can't find land, I'll become her slave, I'll become an entrepreneur. . . ." The dream road continues.

Bottle. What is a bottle? Half the liquid remains. That man seems compelled to examine thicknesses. If this is to follow that conspiracy, what is being tested? The flexure of the fingertip? Nothing, probably nothing. . . . Once I finish drinking it, it's just a light-green bottle. And a soft, strong power works there. It enters "Hell" unexpectedly smoothly. Just half of it disappears into the dark folds.

The drowsiness dodged, the voice and the silhouette had moved to the next room. The room next to the watershed. Here, too, is the wind from the mine coming in. In place of a sandstone candlestick, there also is a horse-shaped wooden figurine. It's the amber-colored horse to which she stretched her hand, calling it *It-hart.*

"Was once a bottle. The beauty of a bottle which no longer is." That half disappears and appears. The smile disappears and appears again.

"So be it. So be it."

But gradually she ceases to smile,

It's still a road. The wind is caressing her hurrying flesh, the wide expanse of her back. Wind from the mine. The mountain far beyond the market, carved white. The road from there to the "examined thickness."

What was once a bottle, what finally has ceased to be a bottle, the woman tries to lay her hand on it, too. And repeats *It-hart, Fore-gib-mi.* Continues to count eternity like a song. (The words whose meanings are not known can't be differentiated.)

Has it finally come halfway? The conspirator who supports the song, his useless busyness. . . . But, the bottle. . . . The bottle is not eternity. Even a woman purchased in a dream, whatever kind of woman she may be, must head for the end of day in a single dash.

The bottle was mercilessly taken out and thrown out beyond her reach. Her hand, as if still groping for the eternal support, crawled about in the remains of the white day, but in time it lost its strength, outstretched, and ceased to move.

The green bottle lying on the floor of reddish bricks. A bottle no one will turn to look upon when "time" passes is just an "examined" substitute. The bamboo blinds are making a quiet sound. The wind from a distant mine caressing the sweaty back of the prostrate woman.

Awakening from dozing, she suddenly mouthed,

"Kokaco-lar."

It was a word he hadn't taught her.

"Kokaco-lar, Kokaco-lar. . . ."

It was like a short song.

The silhouettes of her arms and legs extending loosely.

Coke in a small flower garden in heaven, in a heavenly kingdom.

Or *Kokaco* in hell, a loveable hell.

Kokaco-lar, Kokaco-lar.

I'm not much of a sadist, but my ears are listening, not disliking it.

Kokaco-lar, Kokaco-lar.

Siren Who Disappeared

Bent Arms, Siren's Temptation

Beaubourg, Paris

In all sorts of places angles had been born. A large woman sleeping prostrate. A bathing girl half rising. An old woman with her cheeks on her hands. Young women felling grass and making trees lean. . . . Trace the dreams of the age, and you see in all sorts of places angles had been born.

Women's arms bent shallowly or deeply. Because these are all indexes of dreams that do not cease to win, under a dull sky everyone is talking about angles large and small, eyes closed. Yes, about the victories that have no meaning except when you talk about them.

Siren, Siren with such eyes, you tempt us from dreams. Then everyone becomes talkative. The past is lonely, but the future will be even more lonely. And so meaningless talkativeness never ceases. Siren, as long as your eyes continue to tempt us.

Even when our age began is uncertain. Under the dull sky, everyone is talking about angles large and small, eyes closed. Siren, Siren with such eyes, our future will be even more lonely. Your limpid eyes that drive everyone to meaningless talkativeness. . . .

Green Pebbles

Sandymount, Dublin

Women roaming the beach. Because they were all ghosts with dogs, they disappeared as I passed them. I walked along a narrow strip of sand toward the rocky place at the end of the seashore. Many shadows disappeared, then appeared again. Perhaps they were the same ghosts, the same dogs, but I can't tell.

The Siren, remaining squat on the beach at a distance where she looked as small as a dot, was doing something. I went behind a rock and did "this job," but did not take my eyes off the dot. Lest she be lost among the throngs of ghosts.

As I started to turn back, the dot gradually became the figure of someone facing the other way, her hands touching the sand. Yes, she was picking green pebbles, as if dreaming of "a distance from a distance. . . ." Proteus' summer. The Sandymount strand.

Fragment of a Brick

North Philadelphia

Siren, you need not be afraid even if the giant tree fell soundlessly in the plaza late at night. You need not wake even if a prism that colors death is hung above your bed before dawn. You should go on sleeping, protected by the deep darkness that covers all. But if the merciless Athena advances time and the beauteous morning comes to visit, Siren, you will quietly wake in the seven-colored light that descends through the canopy. Around you there will be countless sacrifices your dreams made playthings of. Not even knowing their meanings, you turn your lovely eyes to a collapsed town, the roots of a giant tree that was felled, shattered glass and bricks.

Siren, you will quietly stretch your hand from your bed and pick up a fragment of a brick like a pebble. Not even knowing its meaning, probably smiling gently. The dreams that will no longer be remembered that have disappeared behind the beauteous morning. . . .

But Siren. Were they truly your dreams? Were they the dreams of you alone that the merciless Athena presided over in the darkness and took away along with the daybreak? A shattered brick, mysteriously, is now left with me. Gently touching a fragment of the sacrifice with a faint smudge of blood, I, alone, turn my thoughts to the dreams that have disappeared. The giant tree that falls soundlessly. The town that collapses. A prism that colors death before dawn. . . .

The Seal

Union Square, New York

The seal. The white mark that closes the door to dreams. I left it unerased. The Siren disappeared behind the dreams, leaving only the white sign. As a story, this is inhuman. Trying to break the seal, I couldn't help being afraid. A beautiful refusal like an alluring voice. The cruel sign remains faintly on the pale door.

Tatehata Akira, born in 1947, is a poet who won the prestigious Rekitei New Poet Prize for his first book, *Yohaku no Runner* (Runners in the Margins), 1991. He has since published two more books, continuing to win the admiration of his fellow poets. This selection in English draws from all three books, plus some uncollected poems.

Tatehata is also an international art critic and curator. He has served, among other positions, as Japanese commissioner for Biennale di Venezia in 1990 and 1993; advisor and catalogue text writer for the Kusama Yayoi Retrospective at MOMA in1998; and artistic director for Yokohama Triennial 2001 and Busan (Korea) Biennale 2002.

Hiroaki Sato, born in 1942, has won prizes for his translations from Japanese. Among his recent books is *My Friend Hitler and Other Plays of Yukio Mishima* (Columbia University Press, 2002). He also writes "The View from New York," a monthly column for *The Japan Times*.